Everything But the Oink!

❧ A Foodie Quiz ❧

To my three favourite cooks:
Abigail, Francesca and Rose.

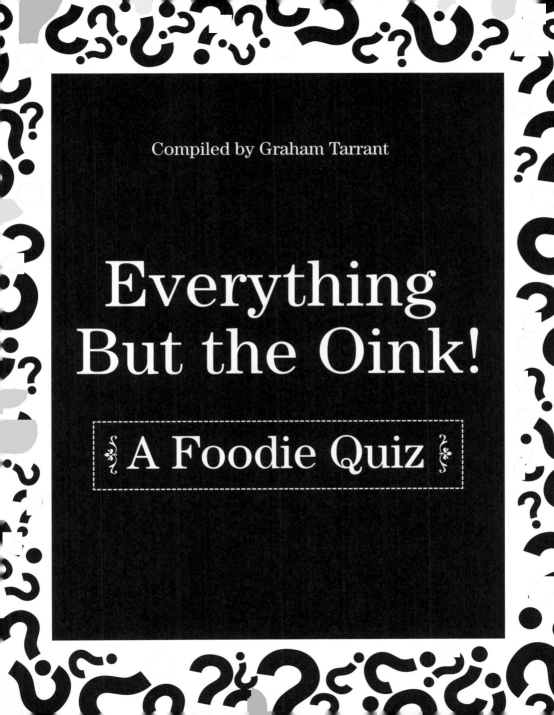

Compiled by Graham Tarrant

Everything But the Oink!

{ A Foodie Quiz }

First published in Great Britain in 2011
by Absolute Press
Scarborough House
29 James Street West
Bath BA1 2BT
Phone 44 (0) 1225 316013
Fax 44 (0) 1225 445836
E-mail info@absolutepress.co.uk
Website www.absolutepress.co.uk

Publisher Jon Croft
Commissioning Editor Meg Avent
Art Direction Matt Inwood
Design Claire Siggery

A catalogue record of this book is
available from the British Library.

ISBN **9781906650605**

Printed and bound on behalf of Latitude
Press in China.

A note about the text
This book was set using the fonts Century,
Rosewoood and Engravers MT.
The first Century typeface was cut in
1894. In 1975 an updated family of Century
typefaces was designed by Tony Stan for
ITC. Rosewood is an ornamental font
designed in 1994 by Kim Buker Chansler,
Carl Crossgrove and Carol Twombly.
Engravers MT was created by Robert
Wiebking in 1899.

CONTENTS

08 AN INTRODUCTION

10 ENGLISH CHEESES
12 WHEN IN FRANCE
14 A LA CARTE (1)
16 TRUE OR FALSE?
18 BODY PARTS
20 SOME THINGS FISHY
22 ADD A SPLASH OF WHAT?
24 COMING TO TERMS
26 SONGS FOR SWINGING COOKS
28 PIECE OF CAKE

30 WHAT'S IN IT?
32 FOOD IN FICTION
34 BY ANY OTHER NAME
36 BANGERS AROUND THE WORLD
38 CELEBRITY DISHES
40 AROUND THE UK
42 TOUCH OF SPICE
44 NUTS!
46 WHO'S WHO?
48 TOOLS OF THE TRADE

50 JAPANESE STYLE
52 WHAT'S WHAT?
54 AS SEEN ON TV
56 ON THE GAME
58 MIXED VEG
60 FOOD AT THE MOVIES : TRAILER
62 SAUCY!
64 A LA CARTE (2)
66 CHINESE COOKY
68 FOOD AT THE MOVIES : MAIN FEATURE

70 WHAT'S COOKING?
72 JUST DESSERTS
74 HISTORICALLY SPEAKING
76 ALL THINGS FRUITY
78 OFF THE SHELF
80 EGGING IT
82 SPEAKING THE LANGUAGE
84 HERBS WISE
86 SIMPLY ITALIAN
88 EVEN FISHIER

90 WHAT'S IN A NAME?
92 HOW WELL DO YOU KNOW YOUR PASTA?
94 SALAD STUFF
96 MISSING PLACES
98 TASTE OF INDIA
100 TERRITORIAL TASTES
102 KITCHEN KNOW HOW
104 SAY CHEESE!
106 A LA CARTE (3)
108 WHO SAID THAT?

AN
INTRODUCTION

Food, glorious food (not a question, though the answer is Lionel Bart's 1960 hit musical *Oliver!*) can be a consuming passion, in or out of the kitchen. For some it is an endless quest for perfection over a hot stove. Others prefer to conduct their research in the chilled-out atmosphere of a gastronomically refined restaurant. Many more studiously follow the step-by-step wizardry of TV's culinary magicians, or feast on course after course in appetisingly presented cookery books. But when rice comes to risotto, how much do we food-lovers actually *know*?

A question is only easy if you know the answer and hard if you don't. The 500 or so questions in this book, tastily arranged into themed sections, will hopefully tantalise, entertain and inform, testing the knowledge of experienced foodies and whetting the appetite of aspiring ones. In short, there's something for everyone – everything, in fact, but the oink.

Good luck – and *bon appétit*!

ENGLISH
CHEESES

1. Blue Stilton can only be legally made in
which three English counties?
2. Which English cheese has a name that might
describe a 'malodorous cleric'?
3. From which English county does Blue Vinny come?
4. How did Double Gloucester get its name?
5. Why is Cheshire known as the 'patriotic cheese'?
6. How does Red Leicester get its distinctive colour?
7. Where did Wensleydale cheese originate?
8. How does Stilton acquire its characteristic blue-veining?
9. What is Lancashire Appledore cheese coated with?
10. Huntsman is a combination of which two English cheeses?

1. Derbyshire, Leicestershire, Nottinghamshire. 2. Stinking Bishop. 3. Dorset. 4. From the original cheese-making method of mixing the evening milk with the following morning's yield. 5. Because it is available in red, while and blue varieties. 6. By adding the natural vegetable dye annatto. 7. France: Cistercian monks accompanying William the Conqueror brought the recipe to England in 1066. 8. During the maturation process the cheese is pierced to allow in air. 9. Cinnamon; it also contains flakes of apple, hence the name. 10. Stilton and Double Gloucester.

1. Which French town is synonymous with mustard?

2. What is a 'gros Bourgogne'?

3. Which new style of cooking became fashionable in France in the 1960s?

4. Truffle hunting traditionally takes place in which season of the year?

5. The vegetable dish ratatouille stems from which region of France?

6. What is *cuisine du terroir*?

7. Nyons in southeast France is famous for its what?

8. How did the *petit four* get its name?

9. What is the name of the mixture of small salad leaves sold in the markets of Provençe and elsewhere?

10. Which Basque ham is named after a local city?

---

1. Dijon. 2. A species of escargot found in Burgundy and elsewhere. 3. Nouvelle cuisine, with its lighter dishes and emphasis on presentation. 4. Autumn. 5. Provence. 6. Cuisine that focuses on regional specialities and local produce, often with a peasant tradition. 7. Olives. 8. *Petit four* means 'small oven' and traditionally these small *pâtisseries* were cooked in ovens that were cooling down after a major bake, utilising what heat was left. 9. *Mesclun*. 10. Bayonne.

WHEN IN

FRANCE

A LA CARTE (1)

1. What does the word 'antipasto' actually mean?
2. With what fruit is a Ripe Tart made?
3. What is the name of the family of Italian hard cheeses made from ewes' milk?
4. Loch Ness, Long Bow and Sprite are varieties of which vegetable?
5. In which country would you eat a carpetbag steak?
6. Which English sausage is traditionally sold by length?
7. Lionel Poilâne, who died in 2002, was celebrated for his what?
8. Which are more nutritious, white or brown eggs?
9. What is a 'Buck Rabbit'?
10. Which famous wartime pie consisted of whatever vegetables were available, mixed with oatmeal and topped with potato pastry?

1. Before the meal. 2. Cherries. 3. Pecorino. 4. French bean. 5. Australia. 6. Cumberland. 7. Bread. 8. There's no difference. 9. Welsh Rabbit (or Rarebit) topped with a poached egg. 10. Woolton Pie, named after the Minister of Food, Lord Woolton.

1. The slaves who built the Egyptian pyramids
were paid in bread.
2. In Russia horseradish is considered to be an aphrodisiac.
3. The American chat-show host Jay Leno trained as a chef.
4. The Chinese dish Chop Suey originated in America.
5. UK consumers eat more chocolate per capita than their
American counterparts.
6. Butter nut is another name for a rock cake.
7. Cat meat masquerading as hare is known as 'roof rabbit'.
8. Eggs are binding for our digestive system?
9. There are more than 1200 varieties of watermelon.
10. The world's first diet book was the work of an undertaker.

1. True. 2. False. 3. False. 4. True. 5. True. 6. True. 7. False. 8. True. 9. True. 10. True. *Entitled Letter on Corpulence Addressed to the Public*, it was written by the funereal William Banting and published in 1862.

TRUE
OR
FALSE?

BODY
PARTS

1. What is the fatty extremity of the rump of a cooked fowl called?

2. When fries are not potatoes what are they?

3. Which part of a calf or lamb is its sweetbread?

4. Why is monkfish seldom sold with its head on?

5. What collectively describes the edible visceral organs of poultry?

6. What is tête de veau?

7. On a crab's body, what are known as 'dead man's fingers'?

8. What colour is cuttlefish ink?

9. The Italian veal dish osso bucco is made with which part of the animal?

10. What are Bath chaps?

---

1. Parson's nose. 2. Testicles of lamb or poultry. 3. Thymus gland or pancreas. 4. Because it's so ugly. 5. Giblets. 6. Calf's head. 7. The grey gills that are removed when preparing the crab. 8. Brown or sepia. 9. Knuckle or shin. 10. The lower portion of a pig's cheeks, cured like bacon.

1. What is a bloater?

2. Which French port is celebrated for its bouillabaisse?

3. What is the correct name for the Dublin Bay Prawn?

4. What is the process of opening an oyster or clam called?

5. Which is the largest marine flat fish?

6. Of what does the South American dish ceviche comprise?

7. What species of fish is a lemon sole?

8. Which fish is considered inedible though its
roe is widely eaten?

9. Are tilapia freshwater or marine fish?

10. Which fish is used to make the Scottish soup Cullen Skink?

1. Herring, salted and lightly smoked. 2. Marseilles. 3. Norway Lobster. 4. Shucking. 5. Halibut. 6. Raw white fish marinated in lemon or lime juice. 7. Flounder. 8. Lumpfish; the roe is used to make imitation caviar. 9. Freshwater. 10. Smoked haddock.

SOME THINGS
FISHY

ADD A
SPLASH
OF WHAT?

Name the alcoholic ingredient traditionally used in the preparation of these dishes.

1. Zabaglione
2. Boeuf Bourguignon
3. Black Forest Gateau
4. Pumpkin Cheesecake
5. Crêpes Suzette
6. Glens of Antrim Stew
7. Soufflé Normand
8. Bäeckeofe (meat stew from Alsace)
9. Bouillabaisse
10. Drunken Crumble
11. Carbonnade à la Flamande
12. Dublin Lawyer (lobster dish)

---

1. Marsala. 2. Red wine. 3. Kirsch. 4. Bourbon. 5. Grand Marnier. 6. Guinness. 7. Calvados. 8. Riesling. 9. Pastis (eg Ricard or Pernod). 10. Whisky. 11. Belgian beer. 12. Irish whiskey.

1. What is a ragoût?
2. How do you blanch something?
3. In the kitchen, what is a liaison?
4. What is the difference between barding and larding?
5. How do you acidulate water?
6. What is a duxelles?
7. Agar-agar is a vegetarian substitute for what?
8. What does it mean to 'macerate' an item of fruit or veg?
9. What are goujons?
10. When is a mixture said to have reached its dropping consistency?

---

1. A meat and vegetable stew. 2. By plunging it into boiling water. 3. Thickening agent such as flour, butter or egg yolk, for soups, sauces and other liquids. 4. With *barding*, strips of bacon or pork fat are placed over poultry or other meat before roasting to prevent it becoming too dry; with *larding*, they are threaded through the meat with a special needle to moisten and boost flavour. 5. By adding a small amount of something acidic, such as lemon juice or vinegar. 6. Mixture of finely chopped mushrooms, onions and herbs, cooked in butter and used as stuffing or to flavour soups and sauces. 7. Gelatine (it is derived from seaweed). 8. To soften or soak in liquid. 9. Strips of white fish or chicken, coated with egg and breadcrumbs and deep-fried. 10. When it is thick enough to fall slowly (ie taking a few seconds) from the back of a spoon.

COMING
TO
TERMS

Fill in the food-related missing words of these song titles.

1. 'Yes! We Have No...'
2. 'Hot...'
3. 'Mean Mr...'
4. 'Mother...'
5. 'On Top Of ...'
6. '...Princess'
7. 'Pour Some... On Me'
8. '... Beret'
9. 'Rockin' Through The...'
10. '... Twilight'
11. 'Sweet Like ...'
12. '... Crawl'

1. What cake takes its name from the Hotel Sacher in Vienna?
2. What ingredients are required to make marzipan?
3. What are Welsh Cakes more commonly known as in Wales?
4. Which British monarch is commemorated in the form of a sponge cake?
5. How did Pound Cake get its name?
6. Which popular light-textured cake is named after the Italian town in which it was first made?
7. What is the mouth-watering structure of the French wedding cake Croquembouche?
8. What type of cake is a Bishop's Cake?
9. What is the German bread-like cake coated in icing sugar?
10. Grasmere in the Lake District is famous for which kind of cake?

1. Sachertorte 2. Ground almonds, sugar and egg whites. 3. Bakestones. 4. Victoria. 5. The original recipe called for 1lb of each of its four ingredients: flour, butter, sugar eggs. 6. Genoise (after Genoa). 7. A cone-shaped tower of profiteroles glazed with caramel. 8. Fruitcake. 9. Stollen. 10. Gingerbread.

PIECE OF
CAKE

WHAT'S
IN IT?

What is the principal ingredient (or ingredients) in each of these traditional British dishes?

1. Stargazey Pie
2. Champ
3. Mock Crab
4. Howtowdie
5. White Devil
6. Poacher's Pie
7. Forfar Bridies
8. Huntington Fidget Pie
9. Likky Pie
10. Tweed Kettle

1. What had a soporific effect on
Beatrix Potter's Flopsy Bunnies?
2. Which small cake triggers the narrator's memory in
Marcel Proust's novel, *Remembrance of Things Past*?
3. What did Hagrid give Harry Potter for Christmas
in his fourth year?
4. Who was served in jail 'very hot buttered toast, cut thick,
very brown on both sides, with the butter running
through the holes in it in great golden drops'?
5. What sandwiches are served in the opening scene of
Oscar Wilde's play, *The Importance of Being Earnest*?
6. The narrator of Salmon Rushdie's novel
Midnight's Children works in a what?
7. What is the final novel in Joanne Harris's 'Food Trilogy'?
8. Oliver Twist asked for more of what?
9. In the classic novel *Moby Dick*, what did Ishmael
and Queequeg eat in the Nantucket tavern?
10. Which Maurice Sendak children's story
has a culinary theme?

---

7. *Five Quarters of the Orange.* 8. Gruel. 9. Clam chowder. 10. *In the Night Kitchen.*
1. Lettuce. 2. Madeleine. 3. Chocolate frogs. 4. Toad in *Wind in the Willows.* 5. Cucumber. 6. Pickle factory.

FOOD IN
FICTION

BY ANY OTHER NAME

How are the following better known?

1. Chinese parsley
2. Arugula
3. Physalis
4. Poor Man's Banana
5. Perpetual spinach
6. Japanese medlars
7. Hickory nut
8. Goober pea
9. Carambola
10. Cow pea
11. Bubbly Jock
12. Indian Fig

1. What is the Spanish sausage lomo made from?

2. The merguez is a native sausage of which country?

3. What shape is the Scottish lorne sausage?

4. Mortadella comes from which Italian city?

5. Which British sausage has cheese as its principal ingredient?

6. In which American city are you most likely to eat chaurice?

7. The British saveloy derives its name from which European sausage?

8. What is the German word for sausage?

9. In which country is a 'sundae' a sausage?

10. What is Australian slang for the common banger?

BANGERS
AROUND
THE WORLD

CELEBRITY

DISHES

1. Which dessert was a tribute to an Australian opera singer?
2. Which English novelist had an omelette named after him?
3. The King Edward potato is named after which British monarch?
4. Which biscuit commemorates a 19th-century Italian patriot?
5. How did the Duke of Wellington prefer his beef?
6. The wife of which US president was famous for her fruit cake?
7. The 17th-century Sally Lunn bun is associated with which English city?
8. Which two rival countries each claim to have created the pavlova?
9. Which classic beef dish is named after a 19th-century composer?
10. Who, in 1899, became synonymous with an oyster dish?

---

1. Peach Melba (in honour of Dame Nellie Melba). 2. Arnold Bennett. While staying at the Savoy Hotel, the writer was so delighted with an omelette created for him by the chef that the hotel decided to put his name to it. 3. Edward VII. 4. Garibaldi. 5. Encased in pastry, hence Beef or Boeuf Wellington. 6. Martha Washington, wife of George and America's first First Lady. 7. Bath. 8. Australia and New Zealand. 9. Tournedos Rossini (after Gioacchino Rossini). 10. US millionaire John D Rockefeller, with Oysters Rockefeller.

1. What is the principal ingredient of laver bread?

2. Which English county is the home of the lardy cake?

3. What is the Liverpudlian dish 'scouse'?

4. In Welsh cuisine, what is a crempog?

5. What is a West Country Hog's Pudding?

6. From which English county does the cheese Yarg originate?

7. What is the name of the pea soup that commemorates the capital city's notorious fogs?

8. What are the spots in a Spotted Dick?

9. In Yorkshire what cake is traditionally eaten on November 5th?

10. What is a Berwick Cockle?

---

1. Seaweed. 2. Wiltshire. 3. Lamb or beef stew. 4. Pancake. 5. Type of sausage. 6. Cornwall. 7. London Particular (ie peasoupers). 8. Usually currants, though sometimes other dried fruit. 9. Parkin. 10. A red and white confectionary associated with Berwick-on-Tweed.

AROUND

THE UK

TOUCH
OF
SPICE

1. What is the most used spice in the world?

2. The word 'clove' means what?

3. By what name is Indian Saffron better known?

4. What is mace?

5. How many spices in allspice?

6. Vanilla is the seed pod of which species of flower?

7. Which spice also goes under the name of 'Devil's Dung', 'Giant Fennel', 'Food of the Gods' and 'Stinking Gum'?

8. Which five spices add up to Chinese Five Spice?

9. What spice is an essential ingredient of Hungarian goulash?

10. The name of which common spice means 'Greek hay'?

1. Black pepper. 2. Nail. 3. Turmeric. 4. Outer covering of nutmeg. 5. One: allspice is the dried unripe fruit of a tree of the same name. 6. Orchid. 7. Asafoetida. 8. Fennel, clove, cinnamon, star anise, Szechuan peppercorn. 9. Paprika. 10. Fenugreek.

1. How do you test the freshness of a whole coconut?
2. What are marrons glacés?
3. What nut is traditionally eaten with Stilton cheese?
4. Macadamia nuts are native to which country?
5. Which nut is principally used to make praline?
6. Why are cashew nuts never sold in their shells?
7. What is sometimes known as a filbert?
8. Which popular 'nut' is not actually a nut?
9. Why are pistachios known in China as the 'happy nut'?
10. Which nuts grow on trees 50m high?

WHO'S WHO?

1. Who published the first of his best-selling food guides in 1957?
2. Who took time out from the movies to co-found the Tribeca Grill restaurant in New York?
3. Who launched their enduring grocery business in London in 1707?
4. Who was the original presenter of television's *Saturday Kitchen*?
5. Who, in 2000, was given the job of improving the quality of food in NHS hospitals?
6. Who stepped off the dance floor and up to the plate?
7. Who was cook in the Bellamy household in the TV drama series *Upstairs Downstairs*?
8. Who made El Bulli in Spain the world's No 1 restaurant?
9. Who made himself synonymous with frozen foods?
10. Who combines writing novels with being a cookery entrepreneur?

---

1. Egon Ronay. 2. Robert De Niro. 3. William Fortnum and Hugh Mason (Fortnum & Mason of Piccadilly). 4. Gregg Wallace. 5. Lloyd Grossman. 6. *Strictly* dancer Anton du Beke, host of the TV cookery show *Step Up to the Plate*. 7. Mrs Bridges (played by actress Angela Baddeley). 8. Chef Ferran Adrià. The restaurant, which is near the Catalonian town of Roses, boasts three Michelin stars. 9. Clarence Birdseye, a New York fur trader in Labrador who observed that fish caught through the ice froze almost instantly in the air and tasted fresh when defrosted and cooked weeks later. 10. Pru Leith, whose novels include such unfoody titles as *A Lovesome Thing* and *Choral Society*.

1. What is a chef's hat called?

2. What name is given to a large pan of hot water in which other dishes are gently cooked or warmed?

3. What is a traditional French stockpot called?

4. What distinctive feature does an oyster knife have?

5. What is a turbotière?

6. A chinois is a type of what?

7. What is a mezzaluna?

8. Which long-handled utensil is heated over an open flame before being used for browning or glazing?

9. What is the function of a cannelle knife?

10. What do you store in a cruchon?

TOOLS
OF THE
TRADE

JAPANESE STYLE

1. What is mirin?

2. Why was seaweed introduced in sushi?

3. Lightly battered, deep-fried seafood and vegetables are called what?

4. What are mushiki?

5. Sakura cheese is flavoured with what?

6. Which Japanese delicacy can be lethal to eat?

7. What is the principal ingredient of the fermented paste miso?

8. Gari is pickled what?

9. Who developed the vegetarian cuisine *shōjin ryōri*?

10. Why should chopsticks never be left standing vertically in a bowl of rice?

---

1. A sweetened rice wine widely used in Japanese cooking. 2. To wrap around the food and thus stop fingers becoming sticky. 3. Tempura. 4. Circular bamboo steamers that can be stacked on top of each other to cook multiple dishes. 5. Mountain cherry leaves (*sakura* means cherry blossom'). 6. Fugu, or 'puffer fish'; its liver in particular is deadly poisonous. 7. Soya bean. 8. Ginger. 9. Buddhist monks. The dishes, which largely consist of rice, tofu and fresh vegetables, have been eaten for centuries by the monks whose religious diet excludes fish, meat or eggs. 10. Because of associations with death (incense sticks are stood upright in sand as part of offerings to the dead).

1. What is a tracklement?

2. What is pastrami?

3. What does the French word vol-au-vent mean?

4. What do you find inside an Eccles Cake?

5. What is a trencher?

6. What are Jolly Boys?

7. What is a gooducken?

8. What is a court bouillon?

9. What is pectin?

10. What is a collation?

1. Savoury jelly served with meat or cheese. 2. Brisket of beef that has been salted and spiced, then coated in peppercorns. 3. Windblown. 4. Currants. 5. A traditional Norman flat loaf on which food was served. Those still hungry could eat the 'plate' as well, hence the term 'trencherman' for someone with a hearty appetite. 6. English pancakes. 7. A goose stuffed with a chicken, which in turn is stuffed with a duck (or sometimes the other way round). 8. Stock used for poaching fish and as a base for fish sauces. 9. Natural substance found in ripe fruits, used as a setting agent for jams and jellies. 10. Light meal.

WHAT'S
WHAT?

1. Who was known as the 'Galloping Gourmet'?
2. *The French Chef* was the title of whose American TV show?
3. Who made his TV debut in the 1998 documentary series *Boiling Point*?
4. Which of 'The Hairy Bikers' was a professional make-up artist?
5. Who was the UK's first celebrity TV chef?
6. Which TV cook was once head chef at Lord's Cricket Ground?
7. In which town did Jamie Oliver start his Ministry of Food campaign?
8. For which international design house was Ed Baines once the official chef?
9. The actor Richard Burton was godfather to which TV chef?
10. What nationality was the chef on *The Muppet Show*?

1. What is gutting a rabbit called?
2. The grouse season traditionally starts on the 'Glorious 12th' of August, but when does it end?
3. What is a squab?
4. Does kangaroo meat have a high or low fat content?
5. Why is jugged hare so called?
6. One is 'Grey', the other 'Red-legged' – what are they?
7. Which berry is most associated with cooking venison?
8. Which French game bird is eaten with a napkin covering the diner's head and face?
9. What is a spatchcock?
10. How should small game birds be hung, by the neck or the feet?

---

1. Paunching. 2. 10th December. 3. Young unfledged pigeon. 4. Low (approx. 2%). 5. The hare was traditionally stewed in an earthenware jug with a sealed lid. 6. Partridges (the larger red-legged species was introduced to the UK from France). 7. Juniper. 8. Ortolan. The intention is to retain the odour along with the flavour, though since the activity is now illegal anonymity may have something to do with it. 9. Game bird (or chicken) that is split open and grilled. 10. Neck (it stops the blood draining from the body and gives the flesh a more gamy taste).

ON THE
GAME

MIXED VEG

1. Mashed potatoes and cabbage are the principal
ingredients of which Irish dish?

2. Swedes and turnips belong to which family of vegetables?

3. Why is the Jerusalem artichoke so called?

4. What colour skin does the root vegetable scorzonera have?

5. Ambercup, Gold Nugget and Sweet Dumpling
are all varieties of what?

6. What is known as the 'oyster plant' or 'vegetable oyster'
because of its taste?

7. What is the difference between snow peas and snap peas?

8. When is a sweet potato not a sweet potato?

9. Finocchio is the vegetable variety of which plant?

10. What were originally known as 'mad apples'
or 'apples of love'?

---

1. Colcannon. 2. *Brassica* (along with cabbage, brussels sprouts, broccoli, cauliflower etc). 3. It has nothing to do with the Middle East. 'Jerusalem' is a corruption of *girasole*, Italian for sunflower, to which the Jerusalem artichoke is related. 4. Black (though the flesh is white). 5. Squash. 6. Salsify. 7. Snow peas, or mange-tout, have flat pods, those of snap peas are rounded. 8. When it's a yam. The two vegetables are often cor fused with one another, though they are quite different species. 9. Fennel (it is also called Florence fennel or sweet fennel). 10. Aubergines – the former because it was thought that eating them would induce insanity; the latter because it was believed they were an aphrodisiac.

Fill in the food-related missing words in these film titles.

1. *Babette's ...*
2. *The ... is Green*
3. *Wild ...*
4. *The ... Train*
5. *The ... and I*
6. *The ... Eater*
7. *Passion ...*
8. *... and Roses*
9. *Paris ...*
10. *Bitter ...*
11. *Eat the ...*
12. *With Six You Get ...*

FOOD AT THE MOVIES:

TRAILER

1. Which sauce made of mayonnaise, gherkins and capers is traditionally eaten with fish?

2. Which two herbs are used to flavour a Béarnaise sauce?

3. What is the term for a sauce made of puréed fruit or vegetables?

4. Which English sauce is typically made with port, gherkins, tongue, mushrooms and hard-boiled egg whites?

5. Satay sauce originated in which country?

6. Guanciale is the principal ingredient in several traditional pasta sauces – what is it?

7. Which French sauce is also known as 'white sauce'?

8. What is the mixture of flour and butter used to thicken sauces called?

9. The word for sauce is the same in both Spanish and Italian. What is it?

10. What turns a hollandaise sauce into a *sauce mousseline*?

---

1. Tartare sauce. 2. Chervil and tarragon. 3. Coulis. 4. Reform sauce. 5. Indonesia. 6. Air-dried pig cheek; nowadays pancetta and prosciutto are often used as substitutes. 7. Béchamel. 8. Roux. 9. Salsa. 10. The addition of whipped cream.

1. What is a Moroccan cooking pot called?

2. Should fresh mussels be open or closed before being cooked?

3. Which famous Parisian restaurant was bought by fashion designer Pierre Cardin in the 1980s?

4. How can you stop bacon from 'spitting' when being fried?

5. Whose many culinary publications included *We'll Eat Again* and *The Spam Cookbook*?

6. Which North African spicy paste comprises red chillies, garlic, caraway seeds, ground cumin and coriander, tomato purée, salt and olive oil?

7. Which fruit was once known as 'butter pear'?

8. What is a bialy?

9. Stuffed chine is a traditional dish of which English county?

10. Who was China's first celebrated gourmet?

---

1. Tagine. **2.** Closed. **3.** Maxim's. **4.** Sprinkle a little salt in the base of the frying pan. **5.** Marguerite Patten's. **6.** Harissa. **7.** Avocado. **8.** A small chewy roll (not unlike a bagel but without the hole), typically topped with onion, garlic or poppy seeds. **9.** Lincolnshire. The pork chine (or backbone) is stuffed with parsley, though other herbs are sometimes added. **10.** Confucius, whose philosophical outpourings embraced fine dining and table manners.

A LA CARTE (2)

CHINESE
COOKY

1. What is 'Chinese cabbage' more generally called?

2. Chow mein is a generic term for a variety of dishes with what as the central component?

3. What is bird's nest soup made from?

4. What is the collective name for the various small savoury dishes traditionally served in Chinese restaurants and tearooms?

5. Name the three principal types of Chinese noodle.

6. Commonly used in Chinese cuisine, what is a water chestnut?

7. What fruit originating in China is sometimes called the Chinese orange?

8. Which Chinese sauce is made from soya beans, vinegar, sugar, garlic, chilli peppers and assorted spices?

9. What in their many different forms are jiaozi?

10. Which celebrated duck dish's name has not kept up with the times?

---

1. Pak choi. 2. Stir-fried noodles. 3. The dried gelatinous lining of the nest of the Asiatic swift and other birds. 4. Dim sum. 5. Egg, wheat, rice flour. 6. The tuber of a variety of sedge grown in paddy fields and marshes. 7. Kumquat. 8. Hoisin sauce. 9. Chinese dumplings. 10. Peking Duck, which is still called that despite the capital's change of name to Beijing.

1. In the film of which literary classic does the eponymous hero work up a sexual appetite while sharing a meal with an equally turned-on companion?

2. What local speciality is on the menu in *Indiana Jones and the Temple of Doom*?

3. Which savoury dish is among Maria's 'favourite things' in *The Sound of Music*?

4. In which Luis Buñuel film is an elegant dinner party constantly interrupted?

5. What do the two canine characters in *Lady and the Tramp* eat for their moonlight dinner?

6. In which film does James Cagney smash half a grapefruit into the face of actress Mae Clarke?

7. Which movie meal for two lasts nearly two hours?

8. In which Charlie Chaplin film is the Little Tramp a guinea pig for a new automated feeding machine?

9. Who explodes from gluttony in *Monty Python's The Meaning of Life*?

10. Name the movie in which a rodent called Remy dreams of becoming a great chef.

---

1. *Tom Jones* (Albert Finney in the title role with Joyce Redman as Mrs Waters). 2. Chilled monkey brains. 3. Schnitzel with noodles. 4. *The Discreet Charm of the Bourgeoisie*. 5. Spaghetti. 6. *The Public Enemy*. 7. *My Dinner with André* (a two-handed conversation piece which takes place almost entirely at the dinner table). 8. *Modern Times*. 9. Mr Creosote (played by Terry Jones). 10. *Ratatouille*.

FOOD AT THE MOVIES:

MAIN FEATURE

WHAT'S COOKING?

Can you identify these well-known dishes from their brief descriptions?

1. Deep-fried chicken breast stuffed with garlic butter.
2. Spaghetti with clams and a white wine sauce.
3. Filet mignon fried in butter, topped with a sauce that includes cream and Worcestershire sauce, then flambéed with brandy before serving.
4. Lobster, parmesan, egg yolks, mustard, sherry or brandy, grilled and served in the shell.
5. Sweet pancake mixture baked with black cherries.
6. Rice cooked with flaked smoked haddock, hard-boiled eggs, garam masala and turmeric.
7. Minced lamb and aubergine casserole, covered with a creamy white sauce and baked.
8. Dessert made of thin layers of puff pastry filled with whipped cream and jam, or fresh fruits.
9. French stew of young spring lamb, potatoes and other root vegetables.
10. A spicy rice dish that includes chicken, prawns, sausage, chillies and tomatoes, cooked Cajun style.

1. Chicken Kiev. 2. Spaghetti alle Vongole. 3. Steak Diane. 4. Lobster Thermidor. 5. Clafoutis Limousin. 6. Kedgeree. 7. Moussaka. 8. Millefeuille. 9. Navarin. 10. Jambalaya.

1. What is the French equivalent of bread and butter pudding?
2. Baklava is made with which type of pastry?
3. What is the predominant flavour in a crêpe Suzette?
4. What is a posset?
5. Can you name the Liverpudlian dessert made from pastry, leftover cake and syrup?
6. What does Eton Mess consist of?
7. Which Italian dessert literally means 'pull me up'?
8. Name the classic French dessert created in honour of Czar Alexander I.
9. Which traditional Scottish dessert is made from oatmeal, double cream and Drambuie?
10. What is the 'black cap' in Black Cap Pudding?

JUST
DESSERTS

HISTORICALLY
SPEAKING

1. In which century was the potato introduced to Britain?
2. What was the name of the famous Parisian food market demolished in 1971?
3. Which English king is said to have died from a 'surfeit of lampreys'?
4. What opened in London on 12 October 1974?
5. Which wartime food item was introduced to the British public in June 1942?
6. Which addition to the English dining table did Thomas Coryate popularise in 1608?
7. Who put the orange colour into carrots?
8. Which popular English cheese is mentioned in the Domesday Book of 1086?
9. What was the favourite vegetable of the 16th-century Catherine de' Medici?
10. What does a well-known variety of lettuce and the Ancient World's most famous physician, Hippocrates, have in common?

---

1. 16th. 2. Les Halles. 3. Henry I, who died in Normandy in 1135 of food poisoning after eating a large portion of his favourite fishy dish. 4. The UK's first McDonald's (in Woolwich). 5. Powdered eggs. One tin held the equivalent of 12 eggs and was the ration for eight weeks. 6. The fork – having seen it widely used during his travels in Italy. 7. The Dutch in the 17th century; prior to that carrots were white or purple. 8. Cheshire. 9. Spinach. When she left her native Florence to marry the future King Henry II of France, she took her spinach-cooking chefs with her and thereafter dishes served on a bed of spinach became *à la Florentine*. 10. Both came from the Greek island of Kos, and hence cos lettuce.

1. From which fruit was sharon fruit horticulturally developed?
2. Ugli fruit is a hybrid of which two fruits?
3. 'Czar' is a popular culinary variety of which fruit?
4. The Granny Smith apple originates from which country?
5. What fruit is blackberry shaped and raspberry coloured?
6. Does a satsuma have pips?
7. Which English vegetable is eaten as a fruit?
8. Which fruit is used to make the Spanish tracklement membrillo?
9. 'Grandee', 'Royal Sovereign' and 'Talisman' are varieties of which fruit?
10. What is a clementine a cross between?

ALL
THINGS
FRUITY

OFF THE
SHELF

1. Which best-selling thriller writer published his *Action Cook Book* in 1965?

2. Whose children's cookbook, *The Fun Food Factory*, became a 1970s TV series?

3. What was the title of Nigella Lawson's first cookery book?

4. Which classic guide to French cooking was first published in 1903?

5. Whose last book, *My Life in France*, was published posthumously in 2006?

6. Who launched her cookery writing career with *Mediterranean Food*?

7. Name the author of the 19th-century English classic, *Modern Cookery for Private Families*.

8. *The Pedant in the Kitchen* relates the culinary experiences of which contemporary English novelist?

9. Which English stately home featured in the title of a 2003 cookbook?

10. Whose *Kitchen Confidential* spills the beans?

---

1. What is a Spanish omelette called?

2. What sauce is a component of Eggs Benedict?

3. In the French dish *oeuf en cocotte* how is the egg cooked?

4. Gulls' eggs are in season in the UK during
which two months?

5. When cooking eggs, what does the term 'over easy' mean?

6. One ostrich egg is the equivalent in weight to
how many standard-sized hens' eggs?

7. When putting it in water, how can you tell if an egg is fresh?

8. What is a coddled egg?

9. Whose recipe for bacon and egg ice cream
initially caused quite a stir?

10. What did Joseph Coyle invent in 1911?

1. Tortilla. 2. Hollandaise. 3. Baked, individually in a small ramekin. 4. April and May. 5. Cooked briefly on the flipside to leave the white firm and the yolk soft. 6. 24. 7. A fresh egg will sink, an old one floats. 8. One that is cooked in water just below boiling point. 9. Heston Blumenthal's (when first served at his restaurant, The Fat Duck). 10. The egg carton.

EGGING
IT

SPEAKING
THE
LANGUAGE

What are the culinary definitions of these familiar foreign words and phrases?

1. *a la plancha*
2. *beurre manié*
3. *al forno*
4. *ghee*
5. *chiffonade*
6. *à point*
7. *farci*
8. *al dente*
9. *mirepoix*
10. *en papillote*

---

1. Grilled. **2.** Kneaded butter: a paste of flour and softened butter to thicken sauces and stews. **3.** Cooked in an oven. **4.** Form of clarified butter used in Indian cooking. **5.** Thin strips or shreds of vegetables, sautéed or raw, served as a garnish. **6.** Medium or medium rare. **7.** Stuffed. **8.** Literally 'to the tooth': when the texture is just firm enough to have some bite, as with perfectly cooked pasta or vegetables. **9.** Mix of finely diced vegetables. **10.** Dish cooked in a greaseproof paper or foil parcel.

1. Which herb is known as 'dew of the sea'?

2. What does borage taste of?

3. In which form is angelica used as a cake decoration?

4. Which four herbs constitute *fines herbes*?

5. What herb is an appetite suppresser?

6. Which herb is used to make pesto?

7. What is unflatteringly known as the 'stinking rose'?

8. What herb adds flavour to the Greek honey of Hymettus?

9. What became known as the 'pizza herb'?

10. In which collection of herbs will you find lavender?

5. Fennel. 6. Basil. 7. Garlic. 8. Thyme. 9. Oregano. 10. *Herbes de Provence*.

1. Rosemary (from its Latin derivation). 2. Cucumber. 3. Crystallised. 4. Parsley, chives, tarragon, chervil.

HERBS

WISE

SIMPLY ITALIAN

1. What does 'ricotta' actually mean?

2. From which part of Italy does cassata ice cream originate?

3. The French call them *cèpes* – what is the Italian name?

4. What colour are cannellini beans?

5. A slice of toasted bread flavoured with oil,
garlic or fat is called what?

6. Which herb is a key ingredient in the veal dish saltimbocca?

7. What is the name of the versatile Italian porridge dish?

8. Which type of pizza is folded and baked with the filling
completely enclosed?

9. Cavallo nero is a variety of what?

10. Which popular Italian dish comprises a mix of meats
boiled in a rich stock?

---

1. What is a pilchard?
2. Ciopinno is a seafood stew associated with which American city?
3. Caviar is the roe of which fish?
4. What is the French fish St Pierre known as in Britain?
5. What is Finnan Haddie?
6. What is brandade de morue?
7. Quahogs are best for making which shellfish dish?
8. What are gefilte fish?
9. Which common flat fish is boneless and scaleless?
10. Which mineral in fish and shellfish is said to be good for the brain?

EVEN

FISHIER

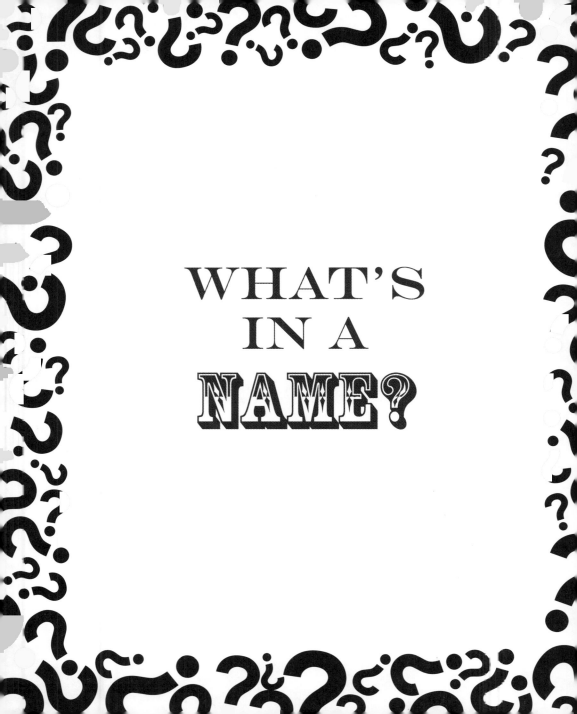

WHAT'S IN A
NAME?

1. In Angels on Horseback, what are the 'angels'?
2. What are hominy grits?
3. In which country did quiche originate?
4. What is the difference between Shepherd's Pie
and Cottage Pie?
5. The word parmentier is applied to dishes containing what?
6. What is a schnitzel?
7. What are Rocky Mountain oysters?
8. Which meat is pease pudding traditionally served with?
9. What is a Penny Bun when it isn't a penny bun?
10. What is a fluffernutter?

---

1. Oysters, wrapped in bacon and served on toast. 2. Coarsely-ground hulled corn. 3. Germany; it was later adopted by the French. 4. Shepherd's Pie is made with lamb, Cottage Pie with beef. 5. Potato (after Antoine Parmentier who introduced the potato to France). 6. Thin cutlet of veal. 7. Buffalo's or bull's testicles (often deep-fried with a cocktail sauce dip). 8. Pork. 9. Wild mushroom. 10. American sandwich made with peanut butter and a marshmallow spread, for those who can stomach it.

1. Which pasta is sometimes referred to as 'Venus's bellybutton'?
2. Name the pasta that is shaped like a butterfly or bow tie.
3. Which pasta takes its name from the Italian hat it resembles?
4. What is pasta *all'uovo*?
5. Why does dried pasta go further than fresh?
6. What is the more common name for 'pasta quills'?
7. What is the meaning of 'vermicelli'?
8. What shape is cannelloni?
9. Which ingredients make up the patriotic colours of fusilli tricolore?
10. How is ruote pasta more popularly known?

---

1. Tortellini. 2. Farfalle. 3. Cappelletti (*cappello* is a hat). 4. Pasta made with eggs. 5. Because it absorbs water when cooked and swells accordingly; fresh pasta requires less cooking and therefore absorbs very little. 6. Penne. 7. Little worms. 8. Tubular. 9. Tomatoes and spinach, with the pasta itself as 'white'. 10. Cartwheel or Wagon Wheel pasta, its shape being that of a six-spoke wheel.

HOW WELL DO YOU KNOW YOUR KNOW YOUR PASTA?

SALAD STUFF

1. What are cucumbers primarily composed of?

2. Radicchio is a variety of what?

3. The leaves of which common garden weed are often used as a salad ingredient?

4. Which salad derives its name from a famous New York hotel?

5. What flavour does the salad herb chervil have?

6. Watercress is a member of which botanical family?

7. Where did the term 'coleslaw' originate?

8. How is a Salade Olivier better known?

9. Which of these is the odd one out, and why: cucumber, radish, tomato?

10. Which lettuce made its first appearance in the UK in the 1970s?

Fill in the missing place names in these geographically inspired dishes.

1. Baked ...
2. ... Mud Cake
3. ... Pork Pie
4. ... Fog
5. ... Coddle
6. ... Pond Pudding
7. Chicken ...
8. ... Flying Fish
9. ... Smokies
10. Tripe à la mode de ...

MISSING PLACES

TASTE OF INDIA

1. What is Bombay duck?

2. What is the difference between pullao and biryani dishes?

3. A raita consists of what?

4. What is the Indian name for cumin?

5. Which is hotter, vindaloo or phall?

6. What does jaggery or gur do to a dish?

7. At what stage of a meal would you normally
eat gulab jamun?

8. What is Indian cottage cheese called?

9. What is the meaning of the word 'mulligatawny',
as in the soup?

10. Gram flour is made from what?

1. A small dried fish. (Bombay duck is also called bummalo). 2. With pullao all the ingredients are cooked together; with biryani the rice is cooked separately. 3. Yoghurt, cucumber and mint. 4. Jeera. 5. Phall. 6. Sweetens it. 7. For dessert. 8. Paneer. 9. Pepper water. 10. Chickpeas.

To which national or regional cuisines do the following dishes belong?

1. Gumbo
2. Lutefisk
3. Soda bread
4. Marmitako
5. Fondue
6. Kushari
7. Fasolada
8. Kalua pig
9. Donburi
10. Tom Yum

1. Creole or Cajun (spicy stew made with meat and/or shrimps). 2. Norwegian (made from dried whitefish, typically cod). 3. Irish (using baking soda as a raising agent instead of yeast). 4. Basque (fish stew, generally with tuna). 5. Swiss (communal dip into melted cheese or chocolate). 6. Egyptian (a dish of pasta, rice and lentils). 7. Greek (bean soup). 8. Hawaiian (traditionally cooked in an underground oven). 9. Japanese (a cooked rice dish; the word actually means "bowl"). 10. Thai (different versions of a traditional soup).

TERRITORIAL
TASTES

KITCHEN
KNOW-HOW

1. When cooking pasta, should the pasta be added to water that is a) boiling, b) simmering, or c) cold and then brought to the boil?

2. How do you shape a quenelle?

3. What is the best utensil for folding whisked egg whites or cream into a mixture?

4. How can you get more juice out of a citrus fruit?

5. Why is crème fraîche an effective cooking ingredient?

6. How do you test the ripeness of a melon?

7. Which is the best way to melt chocolate when cooking?

8. How do you test the freshness of a lobster?

9. Why is steaming the most nutritious method of cooking vegetables?

10. When carving meat, is it best to cut with or against the grain?

---

1. a) Boiling. 2. By smoothing the mixture of finely minced meat or fish (or whatever) between two dessert spoons, thus producing the required oval shape. 3. Large metal spoon. 4. By warming the whole fruit before squeezing it; gently massaging it in your hands can also help. 5. Because it doesn't curdle when heated. 6. Gently press the stalk end of the fruit; if it is ripe it will yield slightly. 7. In a two-tier saucepan: the chocolate goes into the upper compartment, sitting over simmering water in the pan below. Alternatively you can melt it in a bowl resting in a saucepan of water. 8. Lift its tail: it should be stiff. 9. The vegetables are not immersed in water, so they retain more of their nutrients. 10. Against: the meat will look better and be more tender.

1. Mozzarella cheese is made from what?

2. Which cheese is most associated with the Basque region of France?

3. In which US state did Monterey Jack originate?

4. Which has the largest holes, Emmenthal or Gruyère?

5. Which one of the following blue cheeses is made from ewes' milk: Gorgonzola, Roquefort, Shropshire Blue?

6. Windsor Blue is a native cheese of which country?

7. The Scottish cheese Caboc is coated with what?

8. Which British cheese was nicknamed the 'Miners' Cheese'?

9. Which French cheese was known as the 'Cheese of Kings' until the French Revolution, after which it became the 'King of Cheeses'?

10. Which one of these is not an Irish cheese: Crozier Blue, Gubbeen, Munster?

SAY

CHEESE!

A LA CARTE (3)

1. What are the best oranges for making marmalade?
2. In which year was the *Guide Michelin* first published in France?
3. What does cinnamon come from?
4. The egg and lemon soup avgolemono is from which country?
5. Which Hollywood star owns a restaurant called Mission Ranch?
6. What culinary aid did the Swedish Nobel Prize-winning physicist Dr Gustaf Dalen design in 1922?
7. What nationality was the celebrated chef Robert Carrier?
8. What is the banana-like fruit widely used in the tropics as a vegetable?
9. Cilantro is the American word for which herb?
10. Giant Winter Wila, Lyon Prizetaker and Walton Mammoth are varieties of which vegetable?

1. Seville. 2. 1900. 3. The bark of a tree (native to SE Asia). 4. Greece. 5. Clint Eastwood. The hotel/restaurant complex is in his hometown of Carmel in California. 6. The AGA cooker (the name comes from that cf the original manufacturer, Aktiebolaget Gasackumulator). 7. American. 8. Plantain. 9. Coriander. 10. Leek.

1. 'I do not like broccoli. And I haven't liked it since I was a little kid, and my mother made me eat it. I am President of the United States, and I'm not going to eat any more broccoli.'

2. 'I will not eat oysters. I want my food dead – not sick, not wounded – dead.'

3. 'Never eat more than you can lift.'

4. 'How can you govern a country which produces 265 different kinds of cheese?'

5. 'When you cook it should be an act of love. To put a frozen bag in the microwave for your child is an act of hate.'

6. 'Football and cookery are the two most important subjects in this country.'

7. 'Good food is always a trouble and its preparation should be regarded as a labour of love.'

8. 'The only time to eat diet food is while you're waiting for the steak to cook.'

9. 'Never serve oysters in a month that has no pay check in it.'

10. 'When I ask for a watercress sandwich, I do not mean a loaf with a field in the middle of it.'

WHO SAID
THAT?

THANK YOU

It is customary these days for authors to leave a lengthy trail of acknowledgements behind them. However, a list of all the influences behind this little book would outstrip the contents themselves, embracing as it would a lifetime's eating out and in, food shopping expeditions around the world, and a veritable library of nourishing books read and cheerfully digested. There are two things though that have aided and abetted me throughout: a ceaselessly enquiring palate and an appetite that doesn't know when to give in. For each of these I give thanks.